Warriors
Sundra Lawrence

First published 20th May 2022 by Fly on the Wall Press
Published in the UK by
Fly on the Wall Press
56 High Lea Rd
New Mills
Derbyshire
SK22 3DP

www.flyonthewallpress.co.uk
ISBN: 9781913211769
EBOOK: 978-1-913211-93-6
Copyright Sundra Lawrence © 2022

The right of Sundra Lawrence to be identified as the author of this work has been asserted in accordance with the Copyright, Designs and Patents Act 1988.

Typesetting by Isabelle Kenyon. Cover photo author's own.

All rights reserved. No part of this publication may be reproduced, stored in or introduced into a retrieval system, or transmitted in any form, or by any means (electronic, mechanical, photocopying, recording or otherwise) without prior written permissions of the publisher. Any person who does any unauthorised act in relation to this publication may be liable for criminal prosecution and civil claims for damages.

A CIP Catalogue record for this book is available from the British Library.

With thanks to Aryamati Prize sponsors:

Sarah Leavesley
Claire HM
Elisabeth Kelly
Graeme Hall

For my parents

Contents

Rasam	7
Tiger Balm, 1983	8
Somewhere in Normandy	9
Jaffna	10
Summer '95	12
Warriors	14
The Jaffna Public Library of lost books	15
Protests	17
Matriarchs	18
Flame	19
Gold	22
Honeymoon, South Goa	23
Catch	24
Sky walk	25
Grown up	26
Glossary	28

Praise for 'Warriors':

"In Warriors, Sundra Lawrence takes us into Tamil culture, the Sri Lankan civil war, and her life, in language that is tangible, evocative and visceral. There are moments here that will have you holding your breath; moments that will make you smile too. We are indeed 'lucky monarchs' to have these superb poems."
- Rishi Dastidar

"Warriors, Sundra Lawrence's new poetry pamphlet, puts her on the literary map, following in Malika's Kitchen poetic footsteps of Malika Booker's *Pepper Seed* and Jacob Sam-La Rose's *Breaking Silence*. Warriors is part history lesson, part family memoir, part travel diary, all threaded together like a well-fitted jacket. The delicious word choices, the clever line breaks, the riveting stories and the striking lines, like "Cut the island and it will bleed music"- this brilliant short collection makes the reader beg for more." **- Peter Kahn**

"In this stunning book, Sundra Lawrence traces personal and collective histories in the rings of trees, in burning books remembered, in family medicines, in song. These poems find an everyday language for rage and for compassion: they stand as acts of memorial and care." **- Miriam Nash**

"At once personal and public, these beautifully-crafted poems are from the heart and will open hearts. Poems about family, food and love sit alongside poems which are open in telling the truth of the war in Sri Lanka, without brutality or polemic. And every page sings with the love of language." **- Seni Seneviratne, Shash Trevett, Vidyan Ravinthiran (co-editors *Bloodaxe anthology of Sri Lankan Poetry*)**

Rasam

Mum would make it to dry our colds:
Icarus pepper, garam masala,
flesh-soaked tamarind—
sealed with garlic, coriander,
mutton boiled clean off the bone.

You must learn Tamil, speak it!
The swell of heat claps the pot lid,
and sweats our yellow wall.
This is all the medicine you will need
she says, ladling up to brim.

We sit balancing broth on our laps,
blow brown islands in each spoon.
She reminds us not to leave
anything behind. Our tongues burn
pepper hot with each sip.

Tiger Balm, 1983

Why do you have a bomb in your bedroom Mummy?
She says it's a balm and not to play with her things.

I touch the leaping tiger, astride its tin cap detonator.
Daddy calls the Tigers *our only hope*, like Tamil

Obi-Wan Kenobi, fighting for a separate homeland.
Mummy says that I'm too young to know all this.

She untwists the lid, wakens the wax, then laments,
Such a small island, you can't split a tear drop.

Somewhere in Normandy

The dads are dancing. Their wrists, hips
polish the air, metronome feet wake dirt,
lost in *Baila's six-eigthth* beat. It's summer.
Us kids are holding down picnic blankets,
we pick at *sambal* so hot it breaks plastic.
Away from uncle's high-rise outside Paris,
the mums talk Tamil. I listen to its song,
chew straw, suck the memory of orange.

The music of Mozambique slaves, who were
shipped by the Portuguese to fight Lankan kings,
stays in the ear of Sinhalese, Tamil, Burghar,
Muslim, and *Kaffir* Sri-Lankans for all parties.
Before the war, they said Batticaloa Lagoon fish
would sing. Cut the island and it will bleed music.

Jaffna

I. 1989

In the only house with electricity for miles around,
moth-wings scribble the air. Your children are saying
their prayers when the house falls to its knees.

The collapse of concrete floors your body,
dust screeds your face, lines your throat.
Something is wailing, not in your ears.

Get up! Get up! Your children are calling.
One in each arm, you heave your girl and boy,
over broken tiles paid for by your husband,

working as a hospital porter in Saudi
so you can build a home of brick, marble
and rosewood. The gape of night swallows

all sound and insects. Lanterns break curfew
to watch, then help. The mouths of your children
unbuckle, like *Job* in the clasp of prayer.

II.   1991

On receiving the telegram of your father's
sudden death, you prepare to leave.
Jaffna is locked down.

You recall, after the bombing, your father
cycled through night to get to you,
bartered with army and Tiger to get to you.

You sell all your jewellery
to pay for permission to leave.
Heave two children and two suitcases,

trek in Bhatta slippers, feet ploughing
jungle, legs cut and bitten, to reach
where buses start their journey south.

Under a sky of pawned gold,
you three arrive at your mother's door—
your father already hours in the ground.

Summer '95

Returning from a movie in downtown Colombo,
our family is stopped by armed police at a checkpoint.
It's late and we are Tamil. Sinhalese officers poke
a flashlight into the back of the Tuk Tuk.

The driver keeps his hands on the wheel, tries to open
a conversation. A peaked cap officer questions my mum:
Where are you going? Where have you come from?
She answers in rusty Sinhalese. *ID!* he barks.

Mum pulls from her purse a batch of burgundy passports,
places them on top of her oversized black one
the gold letters of *United Kingdom* flare.
The officer opens the Sri-Lankan one first; his torch

picks out the shiny photo and English name.
Place of Birth: Valaan, Jaffna. Silence.
He thumbs the pages of our passports like a royal-
flush, but stops at my brother's childlike shot.

Now 15, his faint moustache seems thicker in this light.
They tell him to step out. Mum pleads, *but we are British*.
I want to shame them with my London vowels.
The officer tells the driver to turn off the engine—

for us to wait in the vehicle. We understand the metal
instruction of rifles. The men encircle my brother;
his shoulders are casual, dark denim,
collar up, like he's hanging with his mates.

Our driver pelts the steering with his fingers
like type-bars, striking a letter of complaint.
Mum pinches each stone of her rosary,
glass beads scratch fast prayer.

My breath is somewhere in the polythene seats.
The officer returns, tips up his cap, rubs the bald crease
above his frown, then asks Mum where she grew up.
Mutawal, Colombo. The surprise unhooks his scowl.

Mutawal, he repeats. His mouth relaxes
on each syllable. *That's where I'm from.* His voice
is song, neighbourhood song and when did she leave?
The passports and my brother are returned.

Please, go straight back to your home.
he slaps the stretched tarp above us,
the gas pedal goes down, the engine climbs
in pitch, like a nest of wasps nearing.

Warriors

After Thomas Schutte's Krieger 2012

We never asked to be made like this,
brutal and injured totems
with the vanity of mountains.
We were acorns once, picked by the sun
and groomed by the wind.
We heard news of the world
carried on the breath of moths.
We took our questions to the sea;
it told us to carry the burden
and broke its mirror over us:
a distillation of everything,
sunrises to burnt stars.
The ground shook, trees yanked
like limbs on a dancing puppet
shaking a map of roots free,
down-pouring rubble and rock.
In that atomic moment, we saw
where hatred and holocaust go,
sealing their rage in our stained bark.

The Jaffna Public Library of lost books

"Where they burn books, they will also ultimately burn people."
- Heinrich Heine (1821)

In 1981, your 100,000 books burnt to black pollen.
Eyewitnesses see police start the fire
and light the fuse for a twenty-six year war.

No mention of the attack in the national press
or the government ministers who bus in thugs,
then watch you burn from their rest houses.

Locals, calf-deep in the hay of singed pages
and ash mounds of sandalwood boxes—
centuries old, salvage what they can.

The lungs of Tamil culture, South Asia's greatest
resource, grown from a collection of ancient texts
the same year that Nazis burned books in Berlin.

In 1983, Jaffna hands rebuild you, months before
war honeycombs your walls with bullets,
then buries your signage with bombs.

Years later, the state reconstructs, repaints, stocks
your shelves. Your students are desperate to study.
Saraswati returns to her pagoda and peonies.

In the diaspora, spines of Tamil books stand unbent
like the tongues of second generation, eyes illiterate
to the swirl of letters, souvenirs of the 100,000 dead.

Protests

"eternity itself will not be long enough to scratch, to even dull, their convex gleam" - Selima Hill*

Sivaramani set fire to her poems,
then killed herself. *Silly girl*, they said.
*She didn't blow up police, or throw in
demands for a Tamil Eelam, and only
twenty-one years old*. Her protest,
in twenty-three poems, survive her.

Kuttimani, handsome and clean-shirted
in the dock, tells of his torture in custody.
He requests that his eyes be donated
to the blind, *so I may one day see Eelam*.
Two years later, his eyes are crow-barred
from their sockets in a high-security prison riot.

The riot passes through like handshakes.
Over two days, Sinhalese prisoners cull
Tamils, cut tongues, tear flesh like mad lions.
One Sinhalese guard protests, tells a skirl
of inmates intent on skinning his Tamil wing,
Over my dead body. No guards are harmed.

---

* *Selima Hill, 'My Uncle's Blazer', Men Who Feed Pigeons (Bloodaxe Books, 2021)*

Matriarchs

The net curtain twitched like it wasn't watching.
I lipsticked my number in the back of your A-Z.
I knew she was ready to drag me out of your car.

The eye cannot see the defect of the eyelid
she said, throwing Tamil parables
before warning, *This is not our culture.*

We ran away on half a tank in your Ford Escort
which served us well until the exhaust fell off on the M1.
We sucked Treble Mints on the hard shoulder.

Your mother cried when you brought
my name home for dinner one Friday night.
It's not personal, you say to me.

Amma will not look at me, she stares
out the window where weeds tiptoe and peep
at dishes that have outgrown the sink.

Flame

I. Holy Communion

Open heart surgery got me off Sunday school.
At Mass, when the others queued for the Eucharist,
I pretended to be a pew, my bone pinned to the beam,
not seeing the stares boring into my nape.

At nine, *Patent Ductus Arteriosus*
taught my parents Latin. Mum's knees grew
wooden from prayer. Dad folded cash
he could not afford in the collection basket.

Ten years later, I rise to give the second reading.
This is the word of God, who sees everything,
a secret boyfriend from a different religion.
I step down from the pulpit and cross my chest.

Lying for love is not truly lying, is it?
The curved scar from under my left breast
to my bra hook burns, as the old walls cry
into their turned-out pockets of holy water.

II. Conversion classes for couples
Ruth 1:16. *Where you go I will go… Your people will be my people and your God my God.*

We sit learning the *Aleph Bet,*
your finger guiding mine from right to left,

I think back to my ancestors, Ceylonese-
Hindu Tamils turned by Catholic missionaries,

perhaps in the 16th century. Tin-roof villages
conquered by spectacular pastel churches

planted on red Jaffna earth; the shade of Amma's
hair, she was home-born at midnight in Velaan.

Midnight babies grow up unafraid, said Grandma.
Cane held tight, Amma chases her naughty brother

into the glove of night, where he tries to hide.
Wherever you go, I'll always follow you, she chides.

My tongue trips on the Hebrew, in this couple's class,
with half of us between the light. Would my people ask

you to convert, bring you to Jesus and church?
We continue, your hand turning the page in reverse.

III. Interview with the Rabbis

"All real living is meeting." - Martin Buber

I told the *Beth Din* that I still believe in Jesus,
and I have questions. They said questions are good.
I told them this is not a conversion, it is an extension
into your world. I don't want to call myself anything,
I'm nearly thirty, and you want to remember the six million.

Gold

The pull of the undertow eases
        your ring clean off,
                while you shake your head laughing.

Our kids help comb the beach for gold,
        clouds of spume tickle their toes,
                your pledge, lost in water's flesh,

falls through tempers of current.
        On another perfect coast, a boy,
                the same age as ours, is found

almost breathing low tide lullabies,
        the sea no longer sick in his belly,
                this island of child, feet

sore from the cut of new shoes,
        Mummy, I can't walk anymore,
                a silent tantrum; red-

soaked t-shirt and undone *Velcro*.
        The detail of his name
                smaller than the photograph—
Alan, not Aylan or *Aurum,*
        hands unclasped, fingers bare,
                on sand he cannot anchor.

Honeymoon, South Goa

We have changed rooms seven times, waking
to high ceilings and the thrum of the Arabian Sea.
My husband wants everything perfect.

A teaspoon of sunlight opens the dawn.
Even before breakfast, flocks of women in
khaki crouch to groom the irrigated grass.

They don't look up or chatter to each other.
We follow the hotel's path to Varca Beach
through the broken gate on the sands,

we are greeted by a swarm of traders
some of whom wear furry Santa hats,
they hold sarongs like tie-dyed spinnakers.

Sir, hello. Excuse me Madam, please!
We give you good price. See, please.
Are you Indian? they ask me,

then stare at my nearly-white husband.
No, I say, firm enough to screw a lid tight.
You too fair for Sri-Lankan, they say to me.

We hold up our soft hands and shake our heads,
walk like Londoners, followed by a trail of batiks,
like the carried cloaks of lucky monarchs.

Catch

My arms outstretched as if hugging sky,
they race to me, grins thicker than the Heath.
"Mummy, Mamma!" I ignore the pull to run
to them, save the seconds that slip into the soil
pushing us closer to the sun. So young, limbs light
and lyrical, soon they will stomp in Autumn,
routine and registration, and listen to the voices
of others. But, for now, there is no homework.
They throw themselves into me, caught and held,
we laugh and kiss, taming the grass as we fall.

Sky walk

Late morning butters the leaf traffic;
a woodlouse is running jobs
in the canyon of an Oak's bark

where even the soil walks differently;
over knuckled roots and mushrooms.
Here, trees bend for each other.

A butterfly lands and parks its wings,
but my in-breath startles it to take off
clapping its way to heaven.

In Baltimore, sneakers slung on top
of lamp posts mark out a drugs drop.
Nearly hidden by the sneeze of spring,

worn out boots sway in the canopy,
like pendulums of hammerless bells
caught in a moment's glance up.

Grown up

Crockery freestyles on the stainless steel—
your clearing-up says I should be helping
and not upstairs practising my pranayama.

Remember your younger words:
I can't resist holding your hand
we squeezed palms under bridges,

watching beakers of gold empty
and dusk spill on our broken clothes
lying in silence, a beg to slow time,

cradling the minutes we had, between
the lies we told our parents and the
two-star hotel off the Harrow Road.

Now, together for seventeen, married
for ten years, anchor your iris to mine;
let us watch this year spring its colour,

bathe in a sky blown clean;
let the land purr with full cups
of sun and washed plates.

Glossary

The Sri Lankan civil war (1983 - 2009) was fought between the Liberation Tigers of Tamil Eelam (LTTE, also known as the **Tamil Tigers**) and the nationalist Sinhalese government.
Harvard International Review 31/8/2020

The LTTE had fought to create an independent Tamil state called **Tamil Eelam** in the north of the island in response to discrimination and persecution against Sri Lankan Tamils.

Baila music is popular to all communities in Sri Lanka. It is most often played at celebrations, and originated from Afro-Sri Lankans and Portuguese. 'Baila is a ballad, in which poetry is paramount. The Portuguese word bailer means 'to dance'. Thuppanhi. https://thuppahis.com/2018/03/29/baila/

Sambal is a hot chilli sauce made with chillies, shrimp, garlic, ginger, onions, sugar and lime juice.

Burghars are a Sri Lankan ethnic group who can trace their roots to Portuguese, Dutch and English colonisers who settled in Sri Lanka.

Kaffirs are Afro-Sri Lankans, who can trace their SriLankan roots to the 16th Century when Portuguese colonisers brought East African slaves to work as labourers and soldiers. The Afro-Sri Lankan community proudly identify as Kaffirs - it is not an offensive term as in South Africa.

Saraswati is the Hindu Goddess of education, wisdom and culture.

The United Nations, estimates that **100,000** people were killed during the conflict.

Kuttimani was one of the founding members of the Tamil Eelam Liberation Organisation, which pre-dates the Tamil Tigers.

Patent Ductus Arteriosus is a persistent opening of two major blood vessels leading from the heart.

The Beth Din is a rabbinical court that decides on conversion to Judaism.

Sky walk In some cultures, shoes tied together and hung from tree branches signify that someone has died. The shoes usually belong to the dead person.

Acknowledgements

My gratitude to those who speak and share stories of survival, even when those stories are ignored or replaced. It is through the telling that we pass on memory and keep it alive. To my Tamil family for their resilience and inspiration, planting their histories in new lands.

I discovered my poetry tribe in my early 20s at Malika's Poetry Kitchen. Twenty years later, many of these writers continue to be dear friends. Special thanks to Anjan Saha and Be Manzini for your generous eyes on these early drafts. Kitchen Alumni family, we make things happen! Patricia, Mervyn, Rajesh, Sandra, Dorothea, Janett. Thanks also to Peter, Charlotte, David, Denise, Jacob, Nick, Roger and Malika. Cath's Poetry Verandah, where I found my Australian writing mates; Coral, Kathy, Mala, Rita and Tineke. To Arji for sound-boarding, Tamar for your art and poetry workshops. To Mimi for your guidance and tutelage. To my talented artist friends Yael and Chinatsu for your enthusiasm. Saradha for your beautiful friendship and support.

Thank you to my mother for her stories and integrity, and my father valuing time and perseverance. Mark, for always being there. Hannah for listening to my poems and always telling me what you think, Isaac for making me laugh and learn. To Aaron, my first reader and soulmate.

Thank you to *Where We Find Ourselves, Arachne Press* and *Inside Out*, for publishing *Summer 95* and *Sky walk*. To Bloodaxe & Apples & Snakes for the original call out that got me on this journey (*poems from the Tamil Diaspora*). To curator Sabrina Jard for selecting Sky walk as an audio art installation (read by Ruth Lass) at the Inside Out exhibition, Shanghai. To the Aryamati Prize and Isabelle Kenyon, Managing Director of Fly on the Wall Press.

Author Biography

Sundra Lawrence was born and resides in north London. She is of Sri Lankan Tamil heritage. Her work often interweaves themes of migration, and conflict and does so with empathy and a deftness of touch. She has performed her work across the UK and internationally. Her poetry and short stories have featured on national television, radio, podcasts, and art exhibitions. They are published in anthologies including the Los Angeles Review. Sundra is the founder and director of Write Lines. She teaches creative writing, and is a creative consultant for the London Literature Lounge. She is a Malika's Poetry Kitchen Alumni.

About Fly on the Wall Press

A publisher with a conscience.
Publishing high quality anthologies, novels, short stories and poetry on pressing issues, from exceptional writers around the globe. Founded in 2018 by founding editor, Isabelle Kenyon.

Some other publications:

The Woman With An Owl Tattoo by Anne Walsh Donnelly
the sea refuses no river by Bethany Rivers
The Prettyboys of Gangster Town by Martin Grey
The Sound of the Earth Singing to Herself by Ricky Ray
Inherent by Lucia Orellana Damacela
Medusa Retold by Sarah Wallis
Pigskin by David Hartley
We Are All Somebody
Aftereffects by Jiye Lee
Someone Is Missing Me by Tina Tamsho-Thomas
Odd as F*ck by Anne Walsh Donnelly
Muscle and Mouth by Louise Finnigan
Modern Medicine by Lucy Hurst
These Mothers of Gods by Rachel Bower
Sin Is Due To Open In A Room Above Kitty's by Morag Anderson
Fauna by David Hartley
How To Bring Him Back by Clare HM
Hassan's Zoo and A Village in Winter by Ruth Brandt
No One Has Any Intention of Building A Wall by Ruth Brandt

Social Media:

@fly_press (Twitter) @flyonthewall_poetry (Instagram)
@flyonthewallpress (Facebook) www.flyonthewallpress.co.uk

About the Aryamati Poetry Prize

This poetry prize remembers Cambridge graduate, Olga Kenyon, (Aryamati), who had a rich career involving teaching, lecturing and writing. She was a well-respected non-fiction author, documenting and researching the history of women's writing and had eight books published. As a keen poet she won the North West Libraries poetry award in 2013 and her poem about Alderley Edge was displayed on the city's trams. This prize seeks poets who write for social change and peace. The prize represents that which Aryamati held dear: reading widely, writing to her loved ones from across the globe by postcard and seeking critical feedback on her work, constantly aiming to improve her craft.

Entry and guidelines:
https://www.flyonthewallpress.co.uk/the-aryamati-poetry-prize

Judge's report on 'Warriors' by Sundra Lawrence:

Spanning 30 years of family history, the content of Lawrence's work proved to be detailed and moving. These poems, exploring civil war in Sri Lanka to modern day London, are incredibly brave and necessary, shining a spotlight on the resilience of the locals, as well as the lingering, multigenerational effects that the brutality of war leaves on people long after they have left their home. We are delighted to be able to publish the debut of Sundra Lawrence, a new shining star in the poetry community.